know your pet

RABBITS

Anna and Michael Sproule

The Bookwright Press
New York · 1988

Know Your Pet

Cats	Rabbits
Dogs	Hamsters

First published in the
United States in 1988 by
The Bookwright Press
387 Park Avenue South
New York, NY 10016

First published in 1988 by
Wayland (Publishers) Limited,
61 Western Road, Hove,
East Sussex, BN3 1JD, England.

© BLA Publishing Limited 1988

Library of Congress Cataloging-in-Publication Data

Sproule, Anna
    Know your pet rabbits/Anna & Michael Sproule
        p.   cm.
    Bibliography: p.
    Includes index.
    Summary: Discusses how to keep a pet rabbit,
covering such aspects as breeding, housing,
selection, care and handling, feeding, and hygiene.
    ISBN 0-531-18217-7
    1. Rabbits as pets — Juvenile literature.
    [1. Rabbits as pets.]
I. Sproule, Michael. II. Title.
SF453.2.S76   1988
636'.9322—dc 19   87-32454
                                      CIP
                                       AC

Designed and produced by BLA Publishing
Limited, East Grinstead, Sussex, England.

A member of the Ling Kee Group
LONDON · HONG KONG · TAIPEI · SINGAPORE · NEW YORK

Photographic credits

t = top, b = bottom, l = left, r = right

cover: Trevor Hill

8 Trevor Hill; 9t Chris Fairclough Picture Library; 9b
Trevor Hill; 10 Stephen Dalton/NHPA; 12t Michael
Huskisson; 12b R.J. Erwin/NHPA; 16, 17, 18, 19, 20,
21t, 21b Chris Fairclough Picture Library; 22t, 22b,
24, 26, 27, 28, 29t, 29b, 30, 32, 33t, 33b, 34 Trevor Hill;
35t, 35b, 36, 37, 40t, 40b, 41, 42, 43t, 43b Chris
Fairclough Picture Library

Illustrations by Derick Bown/Linden Artists; Steve
Lings/Linden Artists; Jane Pickering/Linden Artists
and John Rignall/Linden Artists
Printed in Italy by G. Canale & C.S.p.A. – Turin

Cover: Dwarf varieties like this attractively marked rabbit are extremely popular as pets. They are generally docile animals and make an ideal pet for a child as they can easily be tamed with regular gentle handling.

Title page: The English Lop, one of the oldest fancy breeds, was crossed with various continental breeds to produce the English Dwarf Lop. Like the appealing Dwarf Lop in the picture, they are named after their shorter ears which, unlike those of the French or English Lop, do not reach the ground.

Contents

Note to the Reader

In this book there are some words in the text which are printed in **bold** type. This shows that the word is listed in the glossary on page 44. The glossary gives a brief explanation of words which may be new to you.

Introduction

Rabbits are popular pets for many reasons. They are easy to look after, do not need expensive food, and become friendly to their owners. But, as with other pets, there are questions you should ask yourself before you decide to get a rabbit.

Have you enough time to look after it? Rabbits do not need a great deal of attention, but you must feed them regularly and keep their living quarters clean and **hygienic**.

Do you have space? Rabbits can be kept in a shed, or a hutch in the backyard. They should not be kept inside the house, or in an apartment.

Does everyone in the family agree that owning rabbits would be a good idea? Like all pets, rabbits should only be kept in homes where they will be loved. Remember that once you have bought a rabbit you will be responsible for it for the rest of its life.

▼ A rabbit spends most of its time alone in a hutch outside the house. At least once a day you should take your pet out of the hutch and handle it. Rabbits like being stroked gently and stroking is good for their coats. If you hold your rabbit firmly you can bring it into the house.

8

► The mother rabbit looks very contented with her family. Baby rabbits are born blind and without fur. Although these young rabbits are under four weeks old, their eyes are open and their coats full-grown.

▼ Rabbits like eating greens as well as the pellets you buy from the pet shop. Sometimes your local grocer will give you leftover greens that have not been sold. Remove the dead and yellow leaves before giving these greens to your rabbit. Remove old leaves or stalks that your pet has not eaten from the hutch.

An attractive pet

There are many different breeds and coat colors of pet rabbits. This makes it easy to choose one that you find attractive. As your pet settles down and gets to know you, you will find that it will become friendly. If you are careful, it will let you pick it up and cuddle it. It will learn to come when you call its name.

Feeding and breeding

Rabbits have two main kinds of food—rabbit pellets, which you can buy from a pet shop, and greens, which you can often get free. You can feed your rabbit on wild greens, but you must be careful. Some plants are poisonous to rabbits. You can read about feeding rabbits on pages 30 and 31.

Male rabbits are called **bucks**, and females are called **does**. A doe can produce 25 or more young each year. Rabbit-breeding is an interesting hobby, but do not start it unless you are sure that you have the time, can afford the food, and know of good homes for the young.

About rabbits

The rabbits we have as pets have developed over hundreds of years from wild rabbits. Breeding has made pet rabbits look different from wild ones, but all belong to a group of animals called **lagomorphs**, which means "like hares." Although the rabbit is the same shape as the hare, it is a different **species**.

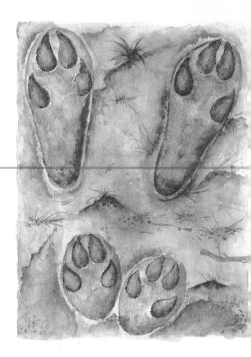

Rabbits and hares

In some parts of the country you may see hares as well as wild rabbits. It is not hard to tell the species apart. Hares are larger than rabbits, with longer legs and slightly redder coats.

Life underground

Rabbits dig their **burrows** in banks and slopes, often near trees where the roots have broken up the ground. They like to live in groups or **colonies**, digging their burrows near each other. Underground, the burrows often join up to form networks of homes and tunnels. These networks are called **warrens**.

▼ In the country, you may see a group of wild rabbits near the edge of a wood. The wood gives them protection from their enemies, and the field gives them grass to eat. Often they burrow around tree trunks. Even if you cannot see any rabbits, look for their marks and droppings.

◀ As rabbits are very timid, you may not often see them in the wild, but you can find their tracks on muddy banks or in damp fields.

▼ Rabbits (*left*) live together in groups. The young are born underground in the rabbit warren where it is safe and warm. Hares (*right*) live in open, grassy places. With their long legs, they can run very fast, sometimes reaching a speed of 65 kph (40 mph). The baby hares are born with furry coats, unlike young rabbits, which are born naked.

Wild rabbits are **nocturnal** animals. They are most active at night. For this reason, you are most likely to see them early in the morning or just before dark. Unless they move, they are not easy to see. The color of their fur matches their surroundings. This helps to protect them from their enemies such as the fox and large birds of prey.

In the wild, rabbits begin to breed when they are about six months old. Wild females can have up to eight **litters** of young each year, with up to eight young in each litter. The young are born blind and without fur. They stay in their burrows for the first weeks of their lives, safely out of the way of enemies, so a large number survive. When the young are old enough, they go off to dig their own burrows and start new families of their own.

Rabbits and people

There are millions of rabbits all over the world, except in the Antarctic. They have spread easily from one country to another. At times, human beings have been responsible for this spread.

The true home of the European rabbit was in Spain and Portugal. When the Roman armies conquered these countries about 2000 years ago the soldiers found that rabbit meat was good to eat. The armies took rabbits with them wherever they went in Europe. Soon there were rabbit colonies in almost every part of the Roman Empire.

Rabbit gardens

The Romans made warrens for their rabbits. These were sometimes called "rabbit gardens," and were surrounded by walls. Later, the rabbit gardens became large rabbit farms. When the Normans invaded Britain about 1000 years ago, they brought the idea of rabbit farming with them. Over the years, so many rabbits escaped and bred that they became a serious problem for farmers, whose crops they damaged and ate.

▲ In the Middle Ages, rabbits were farmed in Britain and all over Europe. This warrener's tower, still standing in Norfolk, England, dates back to the 15th century. It was used as a lookout tower by gamekeepers so that they could keep watch over their rabbit farm.

◄ The Eastern Cottontail is one of many breeds of wild rabbits found in North America. All wild rabbits in North America are descended from those taken there by the first settlers about 400 years ago. The settlers started rabbit farms in their new home country as a source of food.

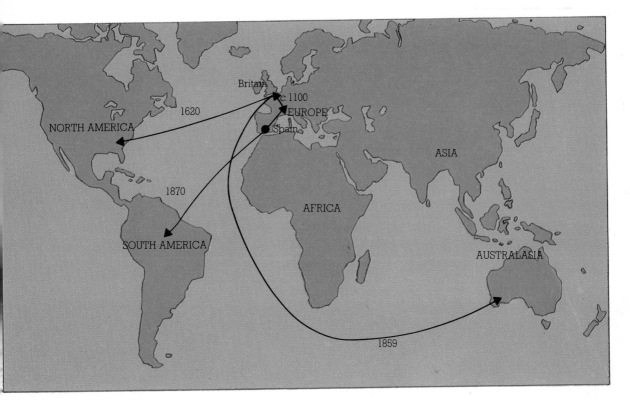

Rabbits throughout the world

There are similar stories about Australia, New Zealand and South America. European rabbits were taken there to breed for meat. They bred so fast, and so many escaped, that they became a serious threat to farming. There were no rabbits in Australia until settlers took just 24 wild European rabbits there in 1859. This was a great mistake. Australia is a farming country, and within a few years the rabbit became one of the Australian farmer's greatest enemies.

There are many kinds of rabbits native to North America. One of them, the jack-rabbit, is really a type of hare. The cottontail is the popular name for a number of other kinds of North American rabbits. As in Europe, pet rabbits and those bred for showing are descended from the European wild rabbit.

▲ This map shows how and when rabbits were taken from Europe by explorers and travelers to other parts of the world. The wild rabbit was well known in Europe nearly 2000 years ago. We know this is true because Roman coins of the Emperor Hadrian have been found bearing the picture of a rabbit.

Rabbit breeds

If you buy a rabbit from a pet shop, it will probably be **crossbred**—that is, a mixture of more than one breed. If you want a purebred specimen, you would do better to go to a breeder who specializes in the breed you want. There are many breeds to choose from, with a number of color varieties in each breed! But a rabbit need not be purebred to make a good pet.

The breeds and varieties have all been developed over the years from the European wild rabbit. Young, healthy rabbits with certain features have been mated with others to produce young with the same features. This is called **selective breeding**.

When rabbits were raised only for meat, it did not matter what they looked like. But when they began to be bred for fur, breeders started to look for rabbits with fur that was dense, strong and of an attractive color.

How breeds differ

Each breed of rabbit is of a particular size and shape. There are two groups of breeds. "Fur" breeds were first bred for the fur trade. "Fancy" breeds are only for show. Fur breeds include the Argenté and Satin. Among the fancy breeds are the Angora and the Flemish Giant. There is room in this book to show only a few of the breeds and color varieties.

▲ Rabbits that are kept as pets have all been developed from the ordinary European wild rabbit.

▼ The Argenté or silvered rabbit is one of the oldest breeds known. This breed, of which there are several color varieties, comes from France where it was well known hundreds of years ago. The variety in this picture is the Argenté Brun. The French words mean "silvered brown" and describe the rabbit's coat.

▲ **The Argenté Champagne is the largest of the Argenté breeds. When seen from a distance, the coat gives the appearance of dull silver.**

An older breed

One of the older breeds is the Argenté, developed in France about 450 years ago. There are four different color varieties, all with French names. The Bleu (blue) has lavender-colored fur tipped with blue. The Brun (brown) has fur tipped with brown. The Crême (cream) has creamy-white fur with orange hairs, and the Champagne slate-blue has fur tipped with silver.

There are different show-standard weights for each variety. The Crême should weigh about 2¼ kg (5 lb), the Bleu and Brun 2¾ kg (6 lb) and the Champagne 3½ kg (7¾ lb).

A selection of rabbit breeds

These are only a few of the breeds and varieties that exist.

Breed	Description and coat	Color	Weight (kg)	Notes
Angora	Soft, silky coat which is spun to make angora wool	White, but also bred in other colors	2¾ (6 lb)	Needs daily grooming
Belgian Hare	Long-legged and very active	Chestnut	4 (9 lb)	Must have plenty of room. Despite its name, it is a rabbit, not a hare
Dutch	Sturdy and lively	Black and white, but other colors are also bred	2¼ (5 lb)	A popular pet breed, easily available
English	Sometimes called English butterfly because of face markings	White with black, blue or other markings	3 (6½ lb)	Popular pet
Flemish Giant	Large and active	Steel-gray	5 (11 lb)	Needs plenty of space
English Lop	Large, with large floppy ears that reach the ground	Various	Up to 9 (20 lb)	Oldest lop-eared breed
Dwarf Lop	Small lop breed. Ears clear of ground	Various	2 (4½ lb)	
Netherland Dwarf	Compact, with rounded ears	Many varieties	1 (2 lb)	Can be kept in small space
Polish	Alert stance with head high	White and various	1 (2 lb)	Easy to handle
Rex	Velvety coat	Various overall (self) colors and patterned and marked vrieties	2½–3½ (5½–7¾ lb)	Needs deep bedding
Satin	Medium size with smooth, glossy coat	Most colors	2½–3½ (5½–7¾ lb)	
Tan	Build similar to wild rabbit	Tan with black, blue, lilac or chocolate back	2 (4½ lb)	Friendly and attractive Good as a pet

Colors and patterns

There are a large number of colors and patterns to be found in almost every breed. This is one reason why keeping pet rabbits is so interesting. If you can arrange it, try to visit a specialist breeder who will show you how the colors and patterns vary.

For showing, the standards, or rules, of coloring and patterning are very strict, but that does not matter if you are only looking for a pet. Breeders often sell young rabbits that do not meet the show standard for their breed, but which make good pets.

Dutch

The Dutch has dark cheeks, ears and hindquarters. The front of the body is white, and there is a white "blaze" on the face. The dark parts can be in many different shades—black, blue, chocolate, gray, yellow or tortoiseshell.

◄ The Dutch is one of the most popular breeds and weighs about 2½kg (5½lb). In spite of its name, this breed first came from Belgium. There are eight different color varieties, the one in the picture being chocolate. It is easy to recognize Dutch varieties. They all have the white "blaze" on the head, a pure white saddle in the front half of the body, and white tips on the hind feet.

Himalayan

The basic color of the Himalayan is pure white, with darker markings, or "points" on the nose, ears, tail and feet. These markings may be black, blue, chocolate or lilac. The eyes are pink. These rabbits make good pets.

The Californian was developed as a breed in the United States and went to Britain in the 1950s. This is a plump breed, with large ears and pink eyes. The body is pure white, and the nose, ears, feet and tail are colored. Weight is about 4 kg (9 lb).

The Harlequin, named after its distinctive checkered coat, was first bred in France in the 1880s, and was originally known as the Japanese.

▲ The English breed is one of the oldest fancy breeds and is very popular both as an exhibition breed and as a foster doe.

Harlequin

The opposing ears, cheeks and feet of the Harlequin are in contrasting colors, with bands of color on the body. The most usual colors are black and orange, but there are also brown and orange, blue and fawn, and lilac and fawn varieties of Harlequins. They are very difficult to breed.

New Zealand White

The New Zealand White is a large rabbit—up to 5 kg (11 lb)—with a pure white coat and pink eyes. The coat is dense and fluffy. New Zealand Whites are docile and make good pets.

English (English Butterfly)

The basic color of the English is white. There is a butterfly-shaped dark area around the nose, with dark patches around the eyes and on the ears, and a chain of dark spots on the body. The dark markings may be black, blue, tortoiseshell, chocolate or gray.

Blanc de Hotot

This very solid-looking breed is all-white except for black rings around its brown eyes. Its normal size is between 4 and 5 kg (9–11 lb), but there is also a dwarf variety.

17

Different coats

The European wild rabbit, from which all breeds have descended, has a fine coat with two layers—the dense, soft **undercoat** and longer **guard hairs**. Over the years, breeders have developed varieties of different coats, some fluffy, some like velvet, some curly.

Rabbits are clean animals and most breeds **groom** themselves to keep their coats clean and free from fleas and other **parasites**. You must always be alert for possible problems with a pet rabbit's coat, but you are not likely to find any.

Angora

If you go to a show, you should not miss the chance to see the Angoras, with their long, fluffy, usually white, coats. Angoras were once greatly prized for their wool, which can be collected and spun into **yarn** to make warm woolen clothes.

The Angora is not a good choice for the first-time rabbit owner, because its coat needs careful and lengthy attention every day.

Chinchilla

Do not confuse the Chinchilla rabbit with the true chinchilla, a squirrel-like animal also kept as a pet. The rabbit has a similar blue-gray coloring. This is in layers—slate blue near the body, then a narrow band of white, and, on the surface, black.

Beveren

Another breed with a thick coat is the Beveren. The oldest color variety is the blue, but there are now also blacks, whites, browns and lilacs. The whites are unusual in having dark eyes, unlike most white rabbits whose eyes are pink.

▲ The Angora breed has been kept for its wool for hundreds of years. Most Angoras are white with large pink or red eyes, but 12 other colors are recognized. Angoras need more grooming than other breeds to make sure that the coat does not become matted. Weight is 2½ to 3 kg (5½–6½ lb).

▼ There are numerous Satin breeds in every variety of color. Satins were first developed in the United States. A breeder noticed a change in coat among a litter of chocolate Havanas. The Satin coat has the appearance and sheen of satin. The English Satin as shown in this picture, weighs from 2½ to 3½ kg (5½–6½ lb).

▲ The Rex varieties, of which there are many, are easily recognized by their velvety coats. The fur is sometimes a little wavy or crinkly. Weight is 2½ to 3½ kg (5½–6½ lb).

Rex Rabbits

In the Rex varieties, the guard hairs do not show up amid the rest of the coat. The fur is short and looks velvety.

Rexes are classed according to the markings of the coat. There are **self** Rexes of one overall color, and there are shaded, patterned and marked varieties.

Satins

If you stroke the coat of a Satin from tail to head, the fur will roll back softly, unlike the more springy coat of other varieties.

The name "Satin" comes from the glossy and silky appearance of the coat. Satins weigh between about 2½ and 3½ kg (5½–6½ lb), and come in many colors.

Shapes and sizes

An adult rabbit weighs anything from 1 kg (2 lb) to a huge 9 kg (20 lb). The larger it is, the larger the hutch it will need and the more room to exercise. So it is important to think about how much space you have for your pet. You should also remember to allow for its growth to full adult size.

If you are a first-time owner, it is best to choose one of the smaller breeds. You can always move on to a larger breed later as you gain experience.

The giant breeds

One of the best known of the giants is the Belgian Hare. It is a true rabbit, but gets its name from its size and its reddish-brown, hare-like coloring. Belgian Hares are active and need plenty of space. Adults grow to about 4 kg (9 lb).

▼ Dwarf breeds weigh only about 1 kg (2 lb). They are therefore very easy to pick up and cuddle. Dwarfs are stocky little rabbits with short stubby little ears. They make ideal companions for guinea pigs, even sharing the same food without fighting.

The Flemish Giant grows to over 5 kg (11 lb). It, too, needs plenty of space. In Britain, the Flemish Giant is usually steel gray in color, but in North America other colors are seen. The American Checkered Giant is even bigger, up to 5½ kg (12 lb). It has "butterfly" markings on the face and black or blue markings on the coat.

The dwarf breeds

At the other end of the scale are the dwarfs. The Netherland Dwarf is a great favorite. It weighs only 1 kg (2 lb) when adult and so makes a good pet for a smaller space. There are many color varieties.

The Polish is a lively and perky dwarf. It is slightly larger than the Netherland Dwarf, at just over 1 kg (2 lb). The most common variety has an overall white coat and pink eyes, but there are other colors.

The Lop

Lop breeds come both large and small. The English Lop is a giant, sometimes growing to over 9 kg (20 lb). The French Lop is smaller, but still classed as a giant. An adult weighs about 5 kg (11 lb). The Meissner Lop is medium sized, growing to about 3 kg (4½ lb).

The Dwarf Lop is the best choice for someone who wants a Lop as a pet. It weighs less than 2 kg (4½ lb), and its ears stay well clear of the ground.

◄ (*above*) **This handsome Belgian Hare, with its long ears and hare-like coloring, is in fact a rabbit, despite its name. It is one of the giant breeds, and adults can sometimes weigh more than 4 kg (9 lb).**

(*below*) **There are several varieties of Lops. All Lops have ears hanging down like the ears of a spaniel. Some Lops are very large, weighing about 9 kg (20 lb). The dwarf, or smaller varieties, like the one in this picture, make very good pets.**

Your rabbit's home

Before you collect your rabbit, its new home must be ready. First, you must decide where its hutch is to go. You can keep rabbits outdoors, except in very cold weather, or you could place the hutch in a shed. Do not use a greenhouse, which will be too hot, or a garage. Exhaust fumes are poisonous.

The rabbit hutch

You can buy a ready-made hutch, or perhaps someone will make you one. It should be as large as possible. The very smallest it should be is 100 cm (39 in) long, 60 cm (24 in) wide and 60 cm (24 in) high, but even a small rabbit will be happier and healthier in a larger hutch.

The hutch must stand on legs, or on a table. There should be two compartments—one, with a wire mesh front, for use by day, and a slightly smaller sleeping compartment. The sleeping part should have a solid front door for cleaning, and a "pop hole" entrance for the rabbit leading from the day compartment.

▲ If you need to, you can stack your hutches one on top of the other. But remember to allow space between them for air to circulate.

◀ Give your rabbit plenty of fresh hay for the sleeping compartment. Change the hay and clean out the compartment at least once a week. Then you will have a healthy and contented pet.

▲ There are many different kinds of rabbit hutches, and some people make their own. There are a few important rules to remember. Give your pet the largest hutch you can afford. The hutch should be escape-proof and easy to clean.

It is useful to have a sliding door to the pop hole so that you can shut one compartment while you clean the other. Cleaning is easier if the floors of both compartments slide out or are fitted with trays that you can remove.

Make sure that the doors of the hutch can be securely bolted from the outside. This will prevent your rabbit from escaping or a dog or fox from getting in to attack it.

Inside the hutch

Your rabbit will need bedding, a food bowl and a gravity-feed water bottle. You can buy special bedding from a pet shop, but sawdust, wood-shavings or straw are just as good. You will need a good supply so that you can change the bedding when you clean the hutch out.

The food bowl should be heavy enough not to tip over. The water bottle will enable your rabbit to drink when it wants to without the risk of making the water dirty or spilling it.

Your pet in the backyard

If your home has a yard with a lawn, you can put your rabbit into an outdoor run during the day. This will give the rabbit a more natural life. It will be able to nibble the grass and get more exercise. Also, you will be able to watch your pet more easily.

There are some precautions you must take. Do not put the run on grass that has been treated with lawn food or weedkiller. Do not use the run on hot days except in a place where the shade will last all day. You should place the run where it can be seen clearly from the house.

An outdoor run

If you buy a run or have one built, make sure that it is completely escape-proof. The best type is shown in the picture on page 25. It has a triangular top and is made of wire mesh on a wooden frame. There is a wire mesh floor so that the rabbit cannot escape by burrowing. Some runs have a sleeping compartment at one end.

▼ Your pet rabbit must not spend all its life caged up in the hutch. On a nice day, you can put it in an outdoor run. The rabbit will be happy to nibble at the grass through the wire mesh floor. Remember to give your rabbit water while it is in the outdoor run.

Moving the run

If you use the run regularly, you will have to move it every day. Then there will be fresh grass for your rabbit to nibble through the wire mesh floor. Move the run before you put your rabbit inside. It is a job for two people, one at each end. Check to see that the grass is fresh and does not contain any poisonous plants. In the summer, check to be sure that the run will stay in the shade. If you follow a system in moving the run, your rabbit will keep the lawn cut without mowing!

In the evening, or if the weather gets bad, return your rabbit to its hutch. Do not think that because it has been eating grass it will not need its usual amount of food. Remember to take away any droppings left in the run or on the grass underneath.

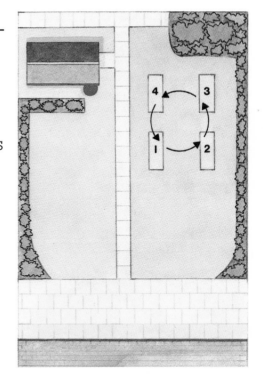

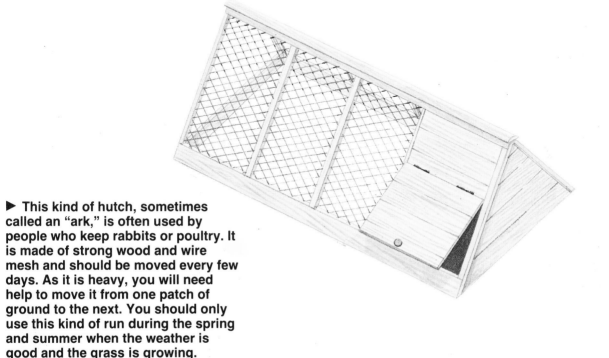

► This kind of hutch, sometimes called an "ark," is often used by people who keep rabbits or poultry. It is made of strong wood and wire mesh and should be moved every few days. As it is heavy, you will need help to move it from one patch of ground to the next. You should only use this kind of run during the spring and summer when the weather is good and the grass is growing.

Choosing your rabbit

Many people get their first rabbit from a friend who has a young rabbit to spare, or has decided to stop keeping rabbits. This is fine as long as the rabbit is in good condition and of the size and sex you want. If not, you will have a better choice if you go to a pet shop or a breeder. Take time to choose, and remember that your rabbit will live for several years.

Making the choice

If you are buying from a pet shop or a breeder, you will be looking for a rabbit at least eight weeks old. It is best to buy in the warmer months. In winter, the change from the warm nest to the cold hutch could be dangerous.

Before you make up your mind, look at all the rabbits that are for sale. If you do not really like any of them, try somewhere else. Before you buy a young rabbit, find out how large the parents are. You need to know if the rabbit you want will fit your hutch.

▼ You can buy your pet rabbit from a pet shop. Before making your final choice, handle several rabbits. Hold the rabbit firmly with one hand under the rabbit's body so that it feels safe. You will soon find a rabbit that you like and that likes you!

Health checks

You must check the health of the rabbit before you buy. If you can, take with you someone who knows about rabbits. Look for bright eyes, a clean, dry nose, and ears that stand up well (except on Lops). There should be no dirt or mess around the tail. Watch the young rabbit moving about and compare the different ones in the **litter**. The liveliest, most inquisitive one is the one to choose.

Bringing your pet home

You will need a carrying box or basket for the journey home. A cardboard one is not much use. Your rabbit will probably jump and twist around, or nibble its way out. If you have a cat's traveling basket or can borrow one, it will do very well. But you should buy a box or basket of your own as soon as you can. You will need it if you ever have to take your rabbit to the vet.

► Taking your new rabbit home from the pet shop is not always easy. Use a cat basket, or, if you must, use a cardboard box with a lid. Put hay in the box and make a few air holes. Do not leave the rabbit in the box for long. It will nibble its way out.

Care and handling

A pet rabbit depends on its owner for its home, food and a happy life. Just as you need love and care from your family, so your pet needs love and care from you—all its life.

Rabbits are not very smart, and you cannot expect your rabbit to respond to you as a cat or dog would. But it will get to know the sound of your voice, and will learn its name if you use it often enough. Talk often to your rabbit. It will not understand what you are saying, but it will enjoy the sound of a quiet, gentle voice.

◄ **You will soon learn how to pick up a rabbit the correct way. With one hand, hold it gently with your hand laid on the scruff of its neck. With the other hand support its rear end. Then lift it up firmly. Make your movements slow and talk to it quietly. Never pick a rabbit up by its ears.**

Handling rabbits

If you learn how to pick up and handle your rabbit correctly from the start, it will not be frightened and will enjoy a gentle cuddling. Never approach a rabbit quickly or jerkily. Always move slowly and gently.

A young rabbit can be picked up in your cupped hands. Take care not to squeeze it as the bones are very delicate. But soon, it will be too big to pick up that way. The correct method then is to put one hand under its bottom to scoop it up and rest the other gently on its ears. Once you have it in your arms you can rest it against your chest—but always keep one hand underneath to take the weight. You must never pick up a rabbit by its ears or the scruff of the neck. If you are handling it correctly, your pet will reward you by staying quietly in your arms, and be happy to be picked up next time.

If you know anyone who has a rabbit, ask to be shown how to pick one up before you buy your own. Handling the rabbit correctly makes all the difference between a friendly, happy pet and a timid or bad-tempered one. But even friendly animals have bad moods. If your pet makes it clear it does not want to be bothered, or has had enough, leave it alone.

▲ Hold a rabbit close to your chest, as in the picture. Support the legs with one hand, making sure the rabbit does not squirm and kick. With your other hand, hold the rabbit around its chest.

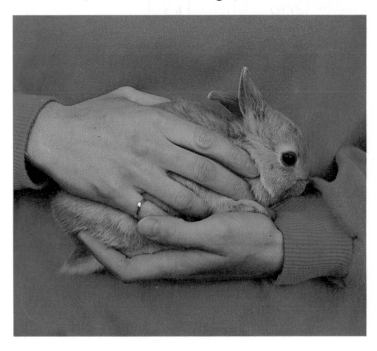

► You can hold a baby rabbit gently in your cupped hands. Do not squeeze the rabbit tightly because its bones are not yet fully grown and are easily harmed.

Feeding

The most important things to remember about feeding rabbits are to feed them at regular times and to make any changes of diet slowly. Like other animals, including humans, they need a mixture of **carbohydrates** for energy, **protein** for growth, **roughage** to aid **digestion**, and **minerals** and **vitamins** for good health. Rabbit pellets, which you can buy from a pet shop, provide some of these things.

Adult rabbits should have a meal every morning and another in the evening. At the same time, the water bottle should be emptied and refilled. Clean the food bowl before each meal.

The morning feeding

It takes only a little time to give a rabbit its meal of pellets, so it is convenient to do this in the morning when time is short. You can fit it in before going to school. Make sure that you leave a full water bottle, because the pellets will make your pet thirsty. Ask at the pet shop how much food to give your pet.

Wild plants

These are some of the wild plants a rabbit can eat:

blackberry (bramble) leaves— but check for thorns

chickweed

wild grasses

dandelion leaves

plantain leaves

sow thistle

clover

◄ You can buy rabbit pellets from the pet shop. These are made up as a complete food specially for rabbits. You will soon learn how much to give your rabbit at each meal. You must make sure your pet has plenty of water. Pellets make rabbits thirsty!

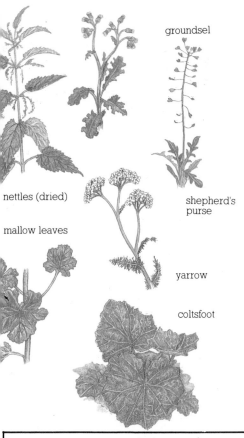

groundsel

nettles (dried)

mallow leaves

shepherd's purse

yarrow

coltsfoot

Greens for your pet

The evening meal will take more time. The main part of this meal is greenstuff. This can be raw cabbage or lettuce left over in the kitchen, together with pieces of raw carrot or turnip. The grocer will often let you have unsold greens for nothing. Try to provide a mixture of fresh food. Too much of any one kind may upset your rabbit.

If there are wild plants near where you live, you can feed your rabbit some of these—but study the pictures carefully. If you are in doubt about any plant throw it away. Save scraps from the house like leftover slices of toast, which most rabbits enjoy. You can also feed such things as small amounts of oatmeal or rice. You will soon find out what your rabbit likes and what it does not. Although rabbits are not fussy about their food, they will leave things they do not like.

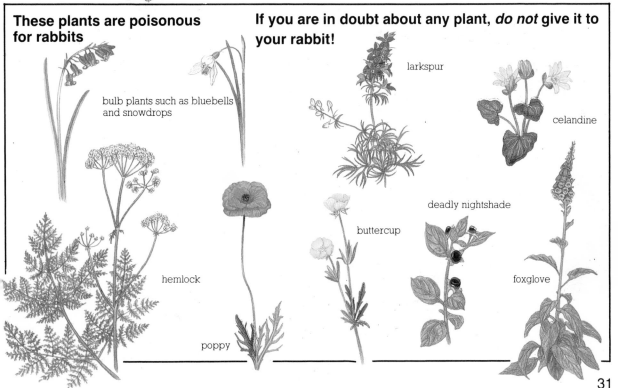

These plants are poisonous for rabbits

If you are in doubt about any plant, *do not* give it to your rabbit!

bulb plants such as bluebells and snowdrops

larkspur

celandine

deadly nightshade

buttercup

hemlock

poppy

foxglove

Cleaning and grooming

Rabbits are clean animals, and they like to live in clean surroundings. One of your duties as a rabbit-owner is to make sure that the hutch is kept clean. Always wash your hands before and after cleaning and grooming!

Check every day for any unwanted food in the hutch, and take it away. Rabbits usually leave their droppings in one corner of the hutch, and these too should be removed daily. Put them on the trash heap if you have one, or with the household garbage. Some rabbits will learn to use a small metal tray as a toilet if it is placed in a corner of the day compartment, well away from the food bowl.

Cleaning the hutch

At least once a week, and more often in hot weather, you should clean the hutch out thoroughly. Shut your rabbit in one part of the hutch while you clean the other, or put the rabbit in its run or traveling box.

▼ Get into the habit of changing the litter at least once a week. Put your rabbit in one compartment while you are changing the litter in the other compartment. Use a garbage bag as shown in the picture.

▶ It is very important to clean out the hutch often. It is not enough just to change the bedding. Use a paint scraper to get right into the corners where there may be rabbit droppings. Hold the dustpan firmly with the other hand as shown in the picture.

Take out the used litter and bedding and put it on the compost heap or in the garbage can. Use a paint scraper or similar tool to scrape off anything sticking to the floor, and sweep the hutch with a brush and dustpan. Put in fresh litter and bedding, and the job is done.

If you ever need to scrub the hutch out, do it on a warm day and make sure the hutch is thoroughly dry before replacing the bedding.

Grooming your pet

Most rabbits, except for Angoras, do their own grooming. But they enjoy being handled by their owners, and a regular grooming session will give you a chance to check on your pet's health. Use a piece of silk cloth or a soft baby brush and brush the coat gently both ways. This will take out any loose, dead hair. Pay special attention to the underneath of the body, where scraps of food or bedding may have stuck to the coat. Keep an eye out for fleas or other parasites, especially in the ears, and check the length of the claws. You can find out how to clip these on page 35.

▼ This Lop enjoys being groomed by its owner. She holds the rabbit with one hand. At the same time, she grooms the rabbit head to tail using a soft brush.

Health care

Given a healthy diet and a clean, snug hutch to live in, your rabbit should stay fit, living up to ten years. But keep the address and phone number of your local vet handy in case you ever need it.

Rabbits need to gnaw something to keep their teeth in good trim. Put a small log in the hutch so that your pet can gnaw the log as often as it likes.

◀ There is probably a vet not very far from where you live. If you are worried about your rabbit, phone the vet and describe what is wrong. You may have to take your pet to the vet. Listen carefully to the vet's advice, and write down the intructions on a piece of paper.

Signs of illness

If your rabbit seems unusually sleepy, stops eating its food, or has a runny nose or eyes, something is wrong. Rabbits' digestion is easily upset, by a sudden change of diet or by eating too much fresh greens, for example. This can cause **diarrhea**—droppings that are runny and smelly—or a condition called **bloat** when the rabbit's stomach swells up. Bloat is usually fatal. However, diarrhea often disappears if you avoid the food that caused the trouble.

This rabbit's teeth have grown too ̇ng. Place a small log in the hutch ̇r your rabbit to gnaw on. After a ̇w weeks, look at your pet's teeth ̇ain. If they are still too long, take ̇e rabbit to the vet.

The most serious of rabbit illnesses is **myxomatosis**, which is spread by fleas. There is no cure, but rabbits can be **vaccinated** against it. If you live in an area where there are wild rabbits with myxomatosis, ask the vet about vaccination.

Another serious rabbit illness is **snuffles**, which spreads easily from one rabbit to another. The signs are like those of a bad cold—runny eyes and nose, sneezing and coughing. The vet can provide a drug that cures most cases. If you have more than one rabbit, move the sick one to separate quarters.

Claw care

Wild rabbits keep their claws trimmed by burrowing, but pet rabbits cannot. They need to have their claws clipped from time to time. This is done with special clippers from the pet shop. You will need the help of an adult if you do it at home. One of you should hold the rabbit while the other clips off a little of each nail at a time. You must only cut the ends of the claws, avoiding the pink part where the blood supply is. If you are worried about this, ask the vet to do it for you.

Your rabbit may have to have its ̇aws clipped from time to time. You ̇n buy clippers from the pet shop, ̇t claw-clipping is not an easy job ̇less you have someone to help you. ̇member that a rabbit's claws will be ̇arper for a few days after clipping. ̇ake sure you do not get scratched!

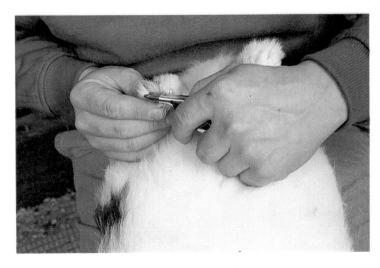

Breeding

When you have kept rabbits for some time you will have learned a good deal about them. You may decide that you want to start breeding. If so, make sure before you start that there are homes for any of the young that you do not want to keep. Remember too that it will be several weeks after the birth before the babies can leave the mother.

Choosing partners

The best time to mate rabbits is in spring or early summer, avoiding cold weather. It is difficult to tell young bucks and does apart, but once they are about six months old you can see the buck's **testes** between its hind legs if you turn it over carefully.

Match the buck and doe with care. You may mate rabbits of different breeds, but the breeds should be similar in size. Mating can take place from about six months onward, but many breeders wait until seven or eight months. Giant breeds take longer to mature and may not be ready to mate until they are nine months old.

▲ The doe should never be mated i her own hutch. The rule is to place the doe in the buck's hutch. Then stand by with a pair of gloves hand If the rabbits begin to fight, put you gloves on and remove the doe.

male

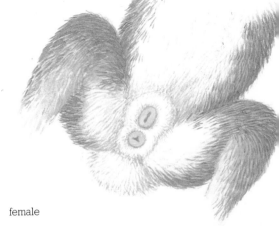

female

You will be able to see when
ating takes place, as in the picture.
appens very quickly, and when it
over the buck falls on his side,
ay from the doe. Then you should
t the doe back in her own hutch.

If you keep rabbits you should
rn how to sex them – that is, to tell
ale from female. Turn the rabbit
er on its back and spread the hind
s. The illustration shows you how
distinguish a male rabbit from a
nale.

Mating

The rule in mating rabbits is to take the doe to
the buck, not the other way round. The buck
and doe may hop around or stamp their feet to
excite each other, or they may mate right
away. Another possibility is that the doe may
refuse the buck, or they may even fight. If
fighting starts, separate the two at once and
take the doe away. Have a pair of gloves
ready so that you do not get scratched. If the
doe refuses the buck, it may be simply that
she is not ready. Try her again in a few hours.

If it is going to take place, mating will happen
very quickly and will soon be over. Afterward,
the buck may fall off on his side, but this is
nothing to worry about. Take the doe away at
once and return her to her own hutch.

Pregnancy and birth

The time between mating a doe and **kindling**—that is, the birth of the litter—is 31 days. You will not be sure whether your doe is **pregnant** until about a week before the birth, but you must start to treat her as if she is. Handle her as little as possible, and when you do so take extra care. Increase her food, but take away any that she does not eat.

Pregnancy

You can buy, or perhaps borrow, a special breeding hutch. This is fitted with a nesting-box and a ledge where the doe can escape from her young when she wants a rest. If your doe stays in her usual hutch, then you should provide a nesting-box which fits inside it. This is a simple wooden box with one low side so that the doe can enter it easily.

Three weeks after mating, give the hutch a final cleaning before the birth. Provide clean, soft bedding and put the nesting-box in place.

▼ When your doe becomes pregnant she is said to be "in kindle." Then you should put her in a breeding hutch, larger than her normal hutch. This will contain a nesting-box in which she will make her nest. There should also be a resting platform for her to use when the young litter begins to become active.

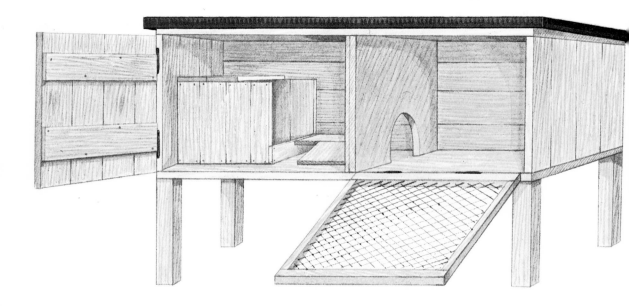

▲ In the breeding hutch the doe will soon start pulling out her fur to line the nest. At this time you will need to give your doe extra food. She will also drink more water than usual.

▼ The doe will give birth to her litter about 31 days after mating. Soon after birth the baby rabbits start feeding on their mother's milk.

About 25 days after mating, the doe will begin to arrange her nest, lining it with fur from her coat. She needs plenty of nourishment now, so give her extras such as bread or breakfast cereal soaked in milk. Make sure that she has plenty of water available. Does become very thirsty as kindling draws near. In the last few days of pregnancy you will see a sharp increase in size.

Birth

Does kindle without help, but as the time approaches you should check often to see how yours is getting on. Keep quiet, and keep strangers and animals away. A day before kindling, most does lose their appetites, sometimes eating nothing at all.

A litter may number from one to twelve, but four to six is more usual. Do not disturb the doe during birth or for at least one day afterward. Then you can examine the nest carefully, after stroking the doe to reassure her and perhaps tempting her away from the nest with a tidbit. You may find one or more of the young, dead. Sometimes the doe will put any dead ones outside the nest.

Rabbits are born blind, deaf and without fur. When you have checked the number, leave the nest as it was and let the doe return to look after her family.

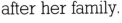

Care of the young

For three weeks after kindling, the doe's milk is all the food the young need. To provide enough milk, the doe needs extra food, and you must see that she receives about three times her normal amount. Keep up the water supply too, using a second bottle or checking and refilling it frequently.

Make sure that there is enough hay or other material to keep the nest warm. The doe may eat some of the hay, so provide more if necessary. It is good to have hay in the nest since, when they are ready, the young will begin to nibble at it and so start to **wean** themselves from the doe's milk.

Fur and eyes

You will be surprised, if you have not seen a litter of young rabbits before, at how quickly they grow. By the fourth day, fur will begin to appear. By the tenth day, the eyes will open. At about two and a half weeks, the young will be ready to take their first steps out of the nest. They will move slowly and nervously at first, but soon they will find that they can hop and jump. Before long they will be running around all over the hutch, and this is the time when the doe will escape to her rest ledge, if she has one, for peace and quiet.

▲ At birth, young rabbits are blind and without fur. When you see a newborn litter for the first time you will wonder how these little things can survive. Do not handle them at all at this stage.

◀ At the age of three weeks, a baby rabbit has all its fur and its eyes are wide open. You can pick it up and nest it in your hands – but not for long. It is still feeding on its mother's milk and depends very much on her.

At about the eighth week, a young rabbit is weaned and is able to look after itself. The mother is no longer important and you can start making friends with it. Touch it and stroke it very gently.

Weaning

Like most young animals, young rabbits are inquisitive. From about five or six weeks on they will taste any food they find in the hutch. That is a sign that they are ready to be weaned. At eight weeks they can be taken away from the doe and put in a separate hutch or taken to their new homes. If you have a spare hutch, put the young in it and leave the doe in her own home.

Newly weaned rabbits should be given three meals a day until they are about twelve weeks old. Feed more pellets and less greenstuff than you would to an adult. It is best to introduce wild greens gradually. If you have any of the young left with you when they are twelve weeks old, you must separate the bucks from the does to prevent them from mating. Telling the sex of young rabbits is very difficult, and you may need the help of an expert.

Showing your rabbit

Going to a rabbit show is a good way of finding out more about the different breeds of rabbits, and you can learn a lot simply by studying the prizewinners. There are big national shows in most countries and many local shows which are smaller but well worth a visit. You can ask at the public library, the local newspaper office, or a nature center to find out if there are any rabbit clubs or shows in your area.

Preparing for the show

You must decide early whether you would like to put your own rabbit into shows, because you may have to register it when it is about six weeks old. To be in a formal show, rabbits must be purebred. Local pet shows are informal and your pet may not have to be purebred for these.

▼ You carry your rabbit to a show in a traveling box. When you get there you check in. You give your name and details about your pet to an assistant. Then the rabbit will be taken out of the box and put in a show pen.

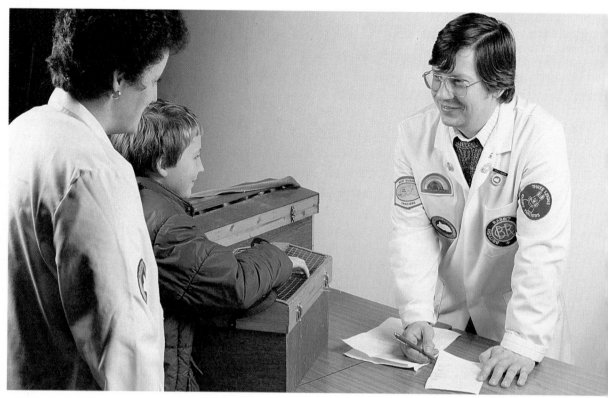

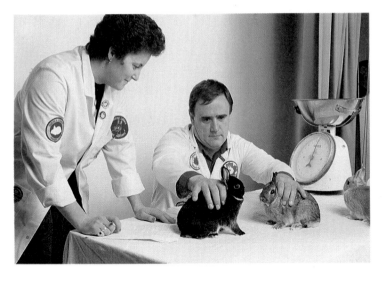

◄ At judging time, a pair of rabbits are placed on a table in front of the judge. The judge checks them for size, weight, coat, color and other important details. Sometimes a judge will see several hundred rabbits in one day's judging.

A show rabbit needs a good deal of preparation. At the show, it will be handled by a judge who will expect it to sit still on the bench while it is examined. It can be trained for this by practice at home with any adults who will help you. If you have friends who show rabbits, ask their advice.

The main equipment you will need for showing is a traveling box. Make sure it has air holes and is easy for you to carry.

At the show

On the day of the show, give your pet a thorough grooming before you leave home. Hay is the best bedding for the traveling box as it is less likely to cling to the rabbit's coat. Take a silk cloth to give the rabbit a final smoothing over before you put it in its show pen.

When the time comes for judging, your rabbit will be taken to the bench. When judging is over, it will be taken back to the show pen. Whether your pet wins a prize or not, you will have had an interesting day and learned a little more about the hobby of raising rabbits.

▼ This fine rabbit has been awarded the first prize for the best English. The English breed is sometimes known as the English Butterfly Rabbit. There are markings either side of the nose that often look like a butterfly's wings. There should be dark markings around the eyes and a dark spot near each eye. The weight should be between 2½ and 3½ kg (5½–7¾ lb).

Glossary

bloat: a serious disease in rabbits; the stomach becomes very swollen. Bloat is usually fatal

buck: a full-grown male rabbit

burrow: a hole in the ground made by an animal as its home

carbohydrate: an energy-giving food, as found in green plants

colony: group of animals living together

crossbred: bred from a male of one pure breed and a female of another pure breed

diarrhea: stomach upset which causes loose droppings

diet: the kinds of food on which a particular species of animal lives

digestion: the process by which an animal converts food to energy

doe: a full-grown female rabbit

groom: to clean and tidy the coat

guard hair: the long hair that shows on the surface of the coat

hygienic: clean and healthy

kindling: the process of giving birth

lagomorph: a mammal that is hare-like in appearance

litter: (1) the young rabbits resulting from one mating (2) sawdust or other material used to cover the floor of the cage

minerals: salts in the diet

myxomatosis: a disease fatal to rabbits

nocturnal: describes an animal that is active by night

parasite: a creature, such as an insect, that lives on another animal

pregnant: describes a female when young are growing inside her body

protein: a substance in certain foods that helps young animals grow

roughage: food such as greens that helps digestion

selective breeding: breeding from a carefully selected male and female in order to produce young with certain looks and qualities

self: (of rabbits) having one overall color

snuffles: an infectious, 'flu-like disease in rabbits

species: a group of animals that are alike in certain ways

testes: the parts of a male body containing sperm for reproduction

undercoat: the fur closest to a rabbit's skin

vaccinated: protected against a disease by an injection

vitamins: substances found in small amounts in food that aid good health

warren: a collection of rabbit burrows

wean: to change the diet from the mother's milk to ordinary food

yarn: wool or cotton thread used in making cloth

Further reading

Choosing Your Own Pet by Mark McPherson. Troll Associates, 1985.
Discovering Rabbits and Hares by Keith Porter. The Bookwright Press, 1986.
Pets by Leda Blumberg. Franklin Watts, 1983.
Rabbits by Fiona Henrie. Franklin Watts, 1980.
Rabbits: All about Them by Alvin and Virginia Silverstein. Lothrop, Lee and Shepard, 1973.
Taking Care of Your Rabbit by Joyce Pope. Franklin Watts, 1987.
Things to Know Before You Get a Pet by Lisa A. Marsoli. Silver Burdett Co., 1985.
You and Your Pet: Rodents and Rabbits by Phil Steinberg. Lerner Publications, 1978.

Index